KEITH A

Every Day

TAKING
ADVANTAGE
OF GOD-GIVEN
OPPORTUNITIES

wesleyan
PUBLISHING HOUSE
wphstore.com

Copyright © 2016 by Keith Alan Loy
Published by Wesleyan Publishing House
Indianapolis, Indiana 46250
Printed in the United States of America
ISBN: 978-1-63257-101-4
ISBN (e-book): 978-1-63257-103-8

This book is revised from the work previously published as *The Bucket List: Making Life Count*, by Keith Alan Loy, 2013, United States of America.

Library of Congress Cataloging-in-Publication Data

Loy, Keith, author.
Every day : taking advantage of God-given opportunities / Keith Alan Loy.
Indianapolis : Wesleyan Publishing House, 2016. | Includes bibliographical references.
LCCN 2016047779 (print) | LCCN 2016049200 (ebook) | ISBN   9781632571014 (pbk.) | ISBN 9781632571038 (e-book)
LCSH: Christian life. | Opportunity.
LCC BV4501.3 .L73 2016 (print) | LCC BV4501.3 (ebook) | DDC   248.4--dc23
LC record available at https://lccn.loc.gov/2016047779

One of my great joys is being a dad. God has blessed me with three of the most amazing girls. Jordan, Jaidyn, and Jaksyn, thank you for filling my life with such joy. Thank you for filling my life with the very breadth of God. Thanks for overflowing my bucket. I love being your daddy.

Contents

For additional free resources, visit
wphresources.com/everyday.

Foreword

Early on, Keith challenges us to "light a fire in our lives." Then, with inspired craftsmanship, he proceeds to counsel us on how to build that fire until it has the impact of true, Spirit-filled wisdom.

Read to be inspired, challenged, and propelled into fulfilling God's call on your life.

Coach Bill McCartney
Chairman Emeritus, Promise Keepers

Live Life to the Fullest

1

My family loves to ride roller coasters. Well, not all of us. My wife's idea of "living on the edge" is watching paint dry. Trust me, she's the love of my life, but she'd rather bob for an apple at a grenade stand than climb aboard a roller coaster of any size. For the rest of us, as Crush (the sea turtle in *Finding Nemo*) would say, "It's righteous!"[1]

I'll never forget the day my daughter, Jaidyn, finally reached the necessary height requirement to cross over into what I call "the joy zone": Disney's Hollywood Studios' Rock 'n' Roller Coaster. She was ecstatic, and for great reason. This bad boy coaster is an indoor, black-lit twister featuring a high-speed launch of 0–60 mph in 2.8 seconds—not to mention Aerosmith blasting through 125 onboard speakers. I screamed like a sissy. As soon as the ride ended I asked my daughter what she thought. With eyes dancing she exclaimed, "That rocked!" No pun intended.

TIME

The fact is, our lives are much like a roller coaster. Every one of us has been launched forward from 0–60 in 2.8 seconds, through twists and turns, soaring up and down. And like any roller coaster, about the time it begins, it's over. As my dad says quite often, "It's a quick trip." I was reminded of that reality when dropping off my eldest daughter at the front door of her high school. It seemed like yesterday that I dropped her off at the entrance of her elementary school. The psalmist wrote: "Lord, remind me how brief my time on earth will be. Remind me that my days are numbered—how fleeting my life is" (Ps. 39:4 NLT).

Have you ever heard the phrase "time flies"? Well, actually it doesn't. In fact, time is one of the few constants we have. Five minutes today is exactly what it was twenty years ago. So it shouldn't surprise you that those same five minutes will be exactly the same twenty years from now. Time doesn't fly, but it does tick away, and it's important you understand that each tick is nonrefundable. Since our days are numbered, don't you think we ought to do our best to make them count?

Perhaps you heard about the clock that was being treated for a nervous breakdown. When the clock master asked him about his troubles, he answered, "Well, I just can't handle life anymore. I mean, look how much ticking I have to do. I tick 120 ticks a minute. That's 7,200 ticks per hour. That's 172,800 ticks per day, 1,209,600 ticks per week, and 62,899,200 per year!" Can you see this clock just wringing his hands?

"Whew, that's a lot of ticks," the clock master replied. "It's no wonder you've been so ticked off lately!" Then he offered this advice: "The way I see it, in order for you to keep on ticking, you're going to have to take each tick one tick at a time."[2]

And we must do the same.

This book is about how we can recapture all that God has purposed and planned for our lives—to live out this life to its fullest. It's a book filled with God's promises in pointing us toward the life he longs for us to live. But to do this, we need to embrace two truths.

NO REGRETS

First, we must decide to live life with no regrets. In other words, make each moment count. Paul wrote in Ephesians, "So be careful how you live. Don't live like ignorant people, but like wise people. Make good use of every opportunity you have" (Eph. 5:15–16 GNT). The fact is, most of us don't make the best use of our time. We'd rather count minutes than embrace moments.

We live life as if we are sitting in a junior high history class. Do you remember watching the clock, wondering if class would ever end? Each minute felt like an hour, and each day felt like a week. Some of you are still counting minutes. You go to work, punch a clock, and then watch it, anxiously awaiting the end of your shift. As each minute ticks away, so does your patience. What we often fail to realize is that each minute is a gift—one to be invested, not endured. Jesus told us that life is to be lived as an adventure: "My purpose is to give a rich and satisfying life" (John 10:10 NLT). In short, we are to live with no regrets.

A popular saying asserts, "Life is not measured by the number of breaths we take, but by the moments that take our breath away." When was the last time you stopped long enough to stand in awe at the majestic hues God paints across the sky during an early morning sunrise? Somehow, somewhere along our journey, we started counting minutes rather than embracing moments. Life became, at best, a routine of endurance, rather than a journey of adventure. Helen Keller wrote, "Security is mostly a superstition. It does not exist in nature, nor do the children of men as a whole experience it. . . . Life is either a daring adventure, or nothing."[3]

Luke's gospel quotes Jesus saying, "To what, then, can I compare the people of this generation? What are they like? They are like children sitting in the marketplace and calling out to each other: 'We played the pipe for you, and you did not dance; we sang a dirge, and you did not cry'" (Luke 7:31–32). In essence, Jesus was saying, "You just sat there. You chose not to experience life; you just endured it. I played the music—you didn't dance. You always wanted to live, but never let yourself. You went through the motion, but never experienced the emotion."

I challenge you to light a fire in your life—to be purposeful about living a life of no regrets. Make every minute count. Savor every moment you get. Take a risk. Make it your personal mission to proclaim with Paul, "I have no regrets" (2 Tim. 1:12 MSG). Take a page out of Peter's book of life and step out of the boat—for it's the only way we'll ever walk on water and be with Jesus. It's important to note that while people often talk about the end of the story where Peter started sinking due to his lack of faith, at least he didn't shy away from trying.

In everything you do, in every word you speak, with every breath you breathe—live, love, and laugh. Plant both feet inside the door of your salvation, and slam the door of routine living behind you. Give Jesus everything you have. Chase him without restraint. I've heard it said that God doesn't give us wings so we can jump; he calls us to jump and *then* gives us wings to fly. Paul wrote to the Christians in Rome, "No one who trusts God like this—heart and soul—will ever regret it" (Rom. 10:11 MSG).

NO REMORSE

The second way we live our lives to the fullest is to love without remorse. The Bible tells us, "Love your enemies. Help and give without expecting a return. You'll never—I promise—regret it. Live out this God-created identity the way our Father lives toward us, generously and graciously, even when we're at our worst" (Luke 6:35 MSG).

Loving without remorse means we learn to just say those loving words of affirmation. Never withhold words that can benefit another. Don't wait for a special occasion like a birthday or anniversary to tell people what they mean to you or how much you appreciate them. Make each moment in someone's day magical, and start doing it today.

If you were to lose a loved one today, be it family or friend, would you be able to say, "We left nothing unsaid"? I strongly urge you: If there is anything you need to say, say it. If there's anything you need to do, do it. Never delay when there's love to say. Put down this book—pick up a phone, write a card, send an email—tell your loved ones they matter. Never leave anything unsaid.

If we're going to love without remorse then we must show it. As a general rule of thumb, any word spoken should be followed up by action. Be high on performance and low on unfulfilled promises. There will always be business to do and deadlines to meet. Don't live your life with good intentions unless you are committed to being intentional about actually doing the good. Show it!

I love to hunt, and part of hunting means taking trips that keep me away from those I love for several days. My wife is amazing, though. Well, actually, she is sneaky. She likes to hide love notes throughout my clothing. And it never fails—I'll be getting ready to hunt, snow is falling, temperatures hover well below zero, and I'll wonder what my family is up to. It is then that I begin to discover those little expressions of love. Those notes have become something I look forward to. How are you at expressing your love to others?

Loving without remorse requires us to share that love. Loving without remorse requires us to share that love. The Bible tells us that we are to share our treasures, not bury them. "It is [ALWAYS] more blessed to give than to receive" (Acts 20:35). I've discovered that those who live life the most—those who are generally the happiest—are also the ones who give the most. We can't take anything with us when we die, so why not spend our living years investing in others?

Let me give you a little challenge when it comes to giving. Though we've likely all heard that no one can ever out-give God—we should try!

GOD'S INTENTION

God intended for *all* of us to live without regrets and love without remorse. It's what Jesus modeled, and it's what Scripture commands. Living this way gives us the confidence to go back and turn our wrongs into rights. It strengthens us to rebuild bridges that we may have once burned. It invites us to revisit love after it has been lost. It removes those "would have/should have/could have" regrets. It turns what may seem gray into ever-defining black and white. It wipes out doubt and fear. It resolves questions and heightens confidences. It always brings about the fullness of life, the joy of living, and the richness of love. It fuels us with great intention and keeps us ever focused on what God desires for our lives.

Solomon once wrote: "Oh, why didn't I do what they told me? Why did I reject a disciplined life? Why didn't I listen to my mentors, or take my teachers seriously? My life is ruined! I haven't one blessed thing to show for my life!" (Prov. 5:12–14 MSG). Life is a quick trip; don't end it full of regret. God intends so much more for our lives than just living in the mundane. He desires that we truly live! And the way we do that is to live without regret and love without remorse.

REFLECT

In what ways am I just enduring life rather than experiencing it? What adjustments can I make?

How can I better express my love to my spouse, my children, my family, and my friends?

Whose intentions am I living for—mine or God's?

Know That You Are Going to Die 2

Everyone needs to know two things about death. First, it's inevitable. You are going to die. Shocking, I know, but it's true. And the last time I checked, the death rate is still hovering around 100 percent (give or take a little). The Bible tells us, "All of us must eventually die. Our lives are like water spilled out on the ground, which cannot be gathered up again" (2 Sam. 14:14 NLT). How uplifting—I'm sure you're just thrilled!

When I was young, I was convinced that I was invincible. Not only did I never talk about death, but I don't even recall ever thinking about it. I was pretty confident that a fine specimen such as myself would never die. But time has a way of changing all that, doesn't it? I still don't think about death much, but my body sure shows me that I'm getting closer to it!

According to the Centers for Disease Control and Prevention, our life expectancy as of 2014 is 78.8 years.[1] Being that I recently turned fifty, and a strapping fifty at that, my life is more than half over. This means I'm not just over the hill, I'm on a downward slide and probably not far from being put underneath it. Death is inevitable, and there is nothing we can say or do that will ever change that.

The second thing to know about death: It's indifferent. It doesn't care who are you. Someone once said that mortality is the great equalizer. It doesn't play favorites, nor does it appeal to selection. When it comes to death, the playing field is equal.

I have a mortician friend who signs every letter with, "Eventually yours." You've got to love that! He's right, though—he will eventually be ours. Solomon wrote, "It's one fate for everybody— righteous and wicked, good people, bad people, the nice and the nasty, worshipers and non-worshipers, committed and uncommitted. . . . Everyone's lumped together in one fate. . . . Life leads to death" (Eccl. 9:2–3 MSG). Now that I've cleared that up, as well as brought some cheer to your life, let me share a little story with you.

UNFULFILLED PURSUITS

Switzerland is known for mountain climbing. People travel from all over the world to experience its ever-popular day hikes. Due to the difficulty of some of the climbs, halfway houses were constructed in which hikers could break for lunch and rest before finishing their trek.

Due to the strenuous first half of the climb, many hikers choose to opt out of the second half in favor of the warmth and comfort of the halfway house. Invariably, as other hikers leave to finish their climb, the ones who choose to stay behind seem happy and talkative. That is, until the hikers' shadows begin to fade, and those who remained make their way to the windows to look up the mountain. Like reading a page from a book, it's written all over their faces—they wish they would have finished their climb.

What I've discovered is that, in life, many make the same choice—to stay in the comfort and easy living of the halfway house. Somewhere in the midst of their life's ascent, they opted out and chose the easy course. And as life's shadows fade, they wish they had continued climbing. How many dreams could have been realized? How many relational conflicts could have been resolved? How many incredible moments have been lost?

God doesn't want us to live with regret, looking up at a mountain wondering "what if." He created us for so much more! The psalmist wrote, "Teach us to realize the brevity of life, so that we may grow in wisdom" (Ps. 90:12 NLT), and this is precisely what we're going to uncover—how to make each moment count.

In Matthew's gospel we read:

When Jesus heard the news about John, he left there in a boat and went to a lonely place by himself. The people heard about it, and so they left their towns and followed him by land. Jesus got out of the boat, and when he saw the large crowd, his heart was filled with pity for them, and he healed their sick.

That evening his disciples came to him and said, "It is already very late, and this is a lonely place. Send the people away and let them go to the villages to buy food for themselves."

"They don't have to leave," answered Jesus. "You yourselves give them something to eat!"

"All we have here are five loaves and two fish," they replied. (14:13–17 GNT)

NEARSIGHTEDNESS

We need to grasp two things if we are to live with no regret and love without remorse—to fulfill God's purposed and planned intentions for our lives. First, we must stop obsessing about what we cannot do and start believing in what God can do. Like a buddy of mine used to say, "Quit whining and start dining."

Look again at the passage in Matthew, "All we have here are five loaves and two fish" (Matt. 14:17 GNT). Nearsightedness is a killer. Obviously they had something far greater than five loaves and two fish. Think about it. The disciples had Jesus—the One who made the fish to begin with. These disciples watched as he opened the eyes of the blind and released the ears of the deaf. Certainly he could super-size a few fish and some bread, right? Think about this in your own life: do you have Jesus?

How often have we missed out on the miraculous because we are so caught up in a mundane circumstance? Jesus is all about putting the super in supernatural. Maybe you're familiar with this poem by Walter D. Wintle: "If you think you are beaten, you are; If you think you dare not, you don't, If you'd like to win, but think you can't, It's almost a cinch you won't. . . . Life's battles don't always go to the stronger or faster man; but soon or late the man who wins is the one who thinks he can."[2]

Have you ever noticed how many limitations we place on ourselves? As the late Charles Schulz once said, "Life is like a ten-speed bicycle. Most of us have gears we never use."[3]

There's a story about a man who died and ran into Saint Peter at the Pearly Gates. (I always love Saint Peter stories.) Immediately the man asked, "Saint Peter, I have been interested in military history for years. Could you tell me who the greatest general of all time was?"

Saint Peter quickly answered, "Well that's simple. It's that man right over there."

"You've got to be mistaken," responded the man. "I knew him. He was just a common laborer like me."

"That's right," replied Saint Peter, "but he would have been the greatest general if he had been a general."[4]

How unfortunate that we are prone to limiting ourselves from doing great things because we can't see past our weaknesses and lose focus of our strengths. If you keep doing what you've always been doing, you'll always get what you've always got. If you keep telling yourself you can't, you most definitely won't. Paul told us that we "can do all this through him who gives [us] strength" (Phil. 4:13). The word *all* in this passage means "all." It doesn't mean some, select, or just a few. It means "all"! Why limit such a resource?

Think about it: if we put limits on what we can do, we put those same limits on what God can do through us. Our God is bigger and more powerful than we can imagine, but we won't experience that if we live like he is small and weak. Jesus said, "According to your faith let it be done to you" and "*all* things are possible" (Matt. 9:29; 19:26, emphasis added). So quit saying, "I can't," and start saying, "I can do all things through Christ." God is limitless; he knows no boundaries—he created stars and galaxies to no end. If he can do that, don't you think he can use you in an unbelievable way?

SELF-CONFIDENCE

The second thing we need to fulfill God's purpose in our lives is to start believing in ourselves. You and I reflect on the outside what we believe on the inside. Life doesn't get better by chance; it gets better by change, and that change begins with a choice. So stop obsessing about what you cannot do. Instead, start believing in what you can do. Or more precisely, what *he* can do.

There's a story about a farm boy from Colorado who loved to hike and rock climb. One day while climbing in the mountains, he found an eagle's nest with an egg in it. He took the egg from the nest, and when he got home, he put it under a hen along with her other eggs.

✳ Since the eaglet hatched among chicks, he thought he was a chicken. He learned chicken behavior from his "mother" and scratched in the chicken yard along with his "siblings." He didn't know any different. Sometimes he felt strange stirrings within, but he didn't know what to do with them, so he ignored or suppressed them. After all, if he was a chicken, he should behave like a chicken.

Then one day an eagle flew over the farm, and the chicken-yard eagle looked up and saw it. In that moment, he realized he wanted to be like that eagle. He wanted to fly high. He wanted to go to the mountain peaks he saw in the distance. He spread his wings, which were much larger and stronger than his siblings'. Suddenly, he understood that he was like that eagle. Though he had never flown before, he possessed the instinct and the capabilities to fly. He spread his wings once more and began to fly. He was unsteady at first, but gained greater power and control. As he soared and climbed through the air, he knew that he had finally discovered his true self.

✳ You may be surprised to learn that I am, in fact, not Michael Phelps. God did not give me a long torso or long arms. I will never swim in the Olympics or win twenty-eight medals—twenty-three of them gold. (I do, however, have eight gold fillings.) But don't feel bad. Truth be told, I don't want to be Michael Phelps. What's the point of investing in a fantasy when I can be myself in reality? Oscar Wilde said it best, "Be yourself; everyone else is already taken."[5] God just wants me to be me, and you to be you.

If we spend our time chasing something we're not, or never could be, we end up forfeiting the joy of being who we are, and what God planned and purposed us to be. If no one else is you, then the world is short a creation God wanted. Why then would you settle for anything less than you?

FAILURE

As we noted in the previous chapter, Jesus "came that [we] may have life and have it abundantly" (John 10:10 ESV). God holds out an offer of abundant living, but we have to reach out and take it. The only thing holding us back is ourselves.

Thomas Edison is one of my heroes—probably because the words *I can't* were never part of his vocabulary. In 1914, when he was sixty-seven years old (don't forget that), his lab, with everything that he had been working on, burned down. Upon seeing the ruins, Edison simply said, "There is great value in disaster. All our mistakes are burned up. Thank God we can start anew."[6] One month later he invented the phonograph (again, he was sixty-seven). By his eighty-fourth birthday, he had invented more than anyone else in recorded history. You see, failure is an inside job. If you don't fail within, you will not fail without. And it's never too late to start believing.

Thomas Edison also said, "If we did all the things we are capable of, we would literally astound ourselves."[7] Remember, whether you think you can or can't, you're always right. I think we need to take on the mindset of famed playwright Neil Simon: "Don't listen to those who say, 'It's not done that way.' Maybe it's not, but maybe you will."[8]

REFLECT

Have I opted for the comfort of the halfway house, or will I finish my climb? Why?

How can I turn my focus away from what I cannot do toward believing in what God can do?

Do I embrace failure as a path to success? If I don't see it that way, how can I change that?

Seize 3 the Day!

Permit me to offer two truths about death. First, all our days are numbered—and we have fewer days today than there were yesterday. You see, death is not a matter of *if*; it's a matter of *when*. David wrote, "LORD, remind me how brief my time on earth will be. Remind me that my days are numbered—how fleeting my life is" (Ps. 39:4 NLT).

The second truth about death is that our days are nonnegotiable. We can negotiate some things in life, but not death. Our departure flight won't be delayed or detoured. As certain was our birth, so is our death. Solomon said, "None of us can hold back our spirit from departing. None of us has the power to prevent the day of our death" (Eccl. 8:8 NLT). Our death has already been placed on God's calendar, and we can do nothing to circumvent that. But hang in there with me—there's good news on the horizon! Our grave doesn't have to mark the end. Paul wrote to believers that our "dying bodies will be swallowed up by life" (2 Cor. 5:4 NLT).

In the book of Romans we discover more key truths for us to embrace:

This is all the more urgent, for you know how late it is; time is running out. Wake up, for our salvation is nearer now than when we first believed. The night is almost gone; the day of salvation will soon be here. So remove your dark deeds like dirty clothes, and put on the shining armor of right living. Because we belong to the day, we must live decent lives for all to see. Don't participate in the darkness of wild parties and drunkenness, or in sexual promiscuity and immoral living, or in quarreling and jealousy. Instead, clothe yourself with the presence of the Lord Jesus Christ. And don't let yourself think about ways to indulge your evil desires. (13:11–14 NLT)

LIVE FOR TODAY

Time is of the essence, so we must learn to live with a sense of urgency. How many times have we read, or heard, about a person who reached the end of his or her life and wondered what happened to all the years, the unfulfilled dreams, the lost opportunities? Such people often are filled with regret thinking about what could have been. Look again at what Paul wrote, "The hour has already come for you to wake up. . . . The night is nearly over; the day is almost here" (Rom. 13:11–12).

One of the most dangerous words in the English language is the word *someday*. Unfortunately, many of us suffer from someday syndrome: *Someday* I'll make things right with my mom. *Someday* I'll have more time for the kids. *Someday* we'll take that vacation. *Someday* I'll talk to my friend about Jesus. *Someday* I'll go back to school. *Someday* I'll. . . . The problem with someday is that it robs us of *this* day. The reality is that someday is really no day at all. The psalmist wrote, "This is the day that the LORD has made; let us rejoice and be glad in it" (Ps. 118:24 ESV).

I read a story about a man who returned to the home in which he once lived after being away for twenty years. He climbed up into the attic and (believe it or not) found an old jacket. Pleased it still fit, he put his hand in one of the pockets and found a receipt for a pair of shoes that he had taken in to be repaired twenty years ago. So, for fun, he went to the shoe shop and handed his receipt to the worker, who then disappeared into the back room. When the worker reappeared, he said to the man, "Come back next

Thursday."[1] Though this might be an extreme case of procrastination, we all know that it's rampant in our world today.

It's time we start living with a sense of urgency, but that does not mean we should start living busier, faster lives. There's a big difference between "urgency" and "emergency." To live with a sense of urgency means we live with an awareness that we are not promised *someday,* and that all we have is *today.* It means we understand that our clock is ticking.

Let me offer you a challenge: Seize the day—specifically, seize *this* day. Don't pass it off or pass it over. Live it, love it, own it. Today might be all you have; tomorrow may never come.

DON'T WASTE TIME

Second, since time is of the essence, we must live with a sense of priority. If you knew you had only a month to live, would you change any of your priorities—those things you deem as essential to your daily life? Of course! We all would. And if we took the time to sift through each moment, we would discover that we waste a lot of time on the unnecessary, wouldn't we? Again, Paul wrote, "The night is almost gone; the day of salvation will soon be here. So remove your dark deeds like dirty clothes, and put on the shining armor of right living" (Rom. 13:12 NLT).

Note Paul's concept of "taking something off" and "putting something on." If we are serious about living with no regrets and loving without remorse, then it's necessary we take off wrong living and put on clothes of right living.

SLOW DOWN

We also must be committed to taking off our hurried pace and putting on a slower one. We need to take off those missed opportunities and put on a measured schedule with room for meaningful moments. We need to take off the need to talk and put on those much-needed ears to listen.

Jesus said, "I have come that they may have life, and have it to the full." But in the first part of that same verse he said, "The thief comes only to steal and kill and destroy" (John 10:10). That's exactly what hurry is—a thief. This thief is killing us by making us run ragged, which causes us to miss moments and opportunities along the way. Carl Jung once wrote, "Hurry is not of the devil; hurry is the devil."[2]

If we rush around, trying to accomplish many things in life, we actually end up robbing ourselves of the truly abundant life. Sounds counterintuitive, doesn't it? Hurry is all about counting minutes; it's never about embracing them. Our need for speed robs us of true joy and ultimately kills us.

What blows my mind is that so many people wear busyness as a badge of honor. Have you ever noticed how people talk?

"How have you been?"

"Busy."

"Yeah? Me too—crazy busy."

It's like a competition where our goal is to "out-busy" each other—that we'll be assumed lazy if we ever said we felt relaxed. Have you ever stopped to consider what is really being said? "I'm too busy to spend time with you." We've turned R and R into running and Red Bull, rather than rest and relaxation.

I assume that if we had only a few days left on earth, we would slow down rather than speed up. We would probably put off those things that clutter our schedules. We would not allow minutes to just pass us by—we would savor every moment. In short, we would make each moment count. I have never been at someone's deathbed and heard them say, "Can you bring me my iPhone?"

The psalmist tells us that God instructs us to "be *still*, and know that I am God" (Ps. 46:10, emphasis added). Did you know that a hurried spirit is actually oxymoronic? We can never follow Jesus at a sprint—following Jesus means we follow at *his* pace.

STOP CHASING THINGS

Taking off our wrong living means we discard our hopeless pursuits. Solomon wrote, "As I looked at everything I had worked so hard to accomplish, it was all so meaningless—like chasing the wind. There was nothing really worthwhile anywhere" (Eccl. 2:11 NLT).

Let me ask a question: On your balance sheet of living, what do you give the most time and attention to—people or possessions? As a society, we spend a vast amount of energy on accumulating things rather than investing in relationships. We spend way too much time, energy, and money investing in the temporal when we ought to be investing in the eternal. Contrary to popular opinion, stuff doesn't pay in the end. The only return on investment worth attaining is the one that comes from investing in the Word and in those around you.

Look at the life of Jesus. He was a master at taking off the wrong stuff and putting on the right stuff—and that right stuff was always people. He spent large blocks of time with his Father and vast amounts of time investing into people. People pay; stuff doesn't.

Jesus noticed an unnoticed tax collector named Matthew. He reached out to a ruthless hustler named Zacchaeus. He touched a blind man named Bartimaeus. He cared about a diseased and desperate woman and gave her the hope she so longed for. He saw and embraced children, who went unnoticed in his day. And, while dying, he even took time to lead one more to his kingdom.

LIVE GOD'S WAY

Let me give you one more challenge when it comes to taking off the wrong stuff and putting on the right: Live God's way. Clothe yourself with his love and his lifestyle. As Paul instructed, "Clothe yourselves with tenderhearted mercy, kindness, humility, gentleness, and patience" (Col. 3:12 NLT). It does not say rush around like a crazy person who chases after things that don't really matter in the end. If you're going to dress for success, make sure you're clothed with a suit tailored by God.

No regrets. No remorse. Live more about today and less about tomorrow. Focus more on people and less on possessions. Live more for God's priorities and less for your own plans.

REFLECT

How often do I make plans for someday rather than for today?
What is one thing I can I do right now to change that?
What, or whom, am I chasing?
In what ways can I slow my pace and walk with God?

Fight 4 Fear

As I've stated several times, we will all die. I know it sounds sobering, but when you truly stop and think about it—strip away the layers and look beyond its grave impression (no pun intended)—it's quite liberating. Think about it: If we are one in Christ, death is just the gateway to something much greater! Paul, quoting Hosea, asked, "O death, where is your sting?" (1 Cor. 15:55 NLT). The answer: the sting of death is swallowed up in Jesus' victory.

Did you know that there are over five hundred different kinds of fears, and that every one of us has at least one? There's the fear of the dark (I have this one), fear of falling, fear of sharks, fear of lobsters. There may even be a fear of falling in the dark on a lobster who thinks he's a shark. Some people fear those frightful words "some assembly required." As it was once affirmed, "The man who knows no fear is not only a gross exaggeration; he is a biological impossibility."[1] The fact is that fear tends to make us do really stupid things and act in really goofy ways.

There's a story about a woman who had just returned home from a trip to Mexico. When she got home, she called her local police department to report that a rattlesnake must have crawled into her overnight bag. The police rushed to the scene. As they carefully unzipped the bag, which was now on the lawn because she threw it out the window in fear, they found the rattlesnake—and discovered it was actually her electric toothbrush.[2]

Alfred Krupp, who was the world's largest weapon producer of his time and thus nicknamed the Cannon King, was, interestingly, afraid of death. He refused to forgive anyone who brought up the subject, and all of his employees were strictly prohibited to speak of it. When a visiting relative of his wife suddenly died, Krupp bolted from the house in terror. Later, when his wife complained about him leaving, he abandoned her.[3]

Former columnist Ann Landers once noted that she would receive an average of 10,000 letters each month. The common thread in all of these letters? Fear. Even the medical industry tells us that 90 percent of the chronic patients they see have one common symptom—fear.[4]

Fear is precisely the reason why we don't experience the abundant life.

FEAR EQUALS LIMITATION

I'm going to highlight several dream busters (or fears) that we often face. They are in no particular order, but each one should be given very careful and special attention. The first is family and friends.

How many times have we had a great idea that we eagerly shared with our family and friends? And what we heard in return was, "What are you thinking? You can't do that! It'll never work!" And how many of those great ideas become abandoned dreams? We give up due to being laughed at by our friends and loved ones. The power of words is absolutely amazing, and it is magnified when it comes from those closest to us. Every time we give up to stay in the good graces of those we love, we actually sacrifice the greater places purposed by the One who loves us most. Have you ever stopped to consider that maybe those far-fetched dreams were actually not your dreams—but the ones God had for you? The Bible says, "'I know the plans I have for you,' says the LORD. 'They are plans for good and not for disaster, to give you a future and a hope'" (Jer. 29:11 NLT).

Another dream buster is the fear of not fitting in—the fear of rejection. No one likes to be rejected, and it's probably why some never risk getting too close to others. The fear can be unbearable. The Bible tells us, "Some 'friends' pretend to be friends, but a true friend sticks closer than a brother" (Prov. 18:24 CJB). Your brother is your brother because he has to be; your friend is your friend because he *wants* to be and will walk through those fears with you.

Avremel Zelmanowitz exemplified what it means to be a *true* friend. He was working in the World Trade Center on that fateful day of September 11, 2001, along with his good friend Ed Beyea. Ed was quadriplegic after having become injured in a car accident when he was twenty-two years old. On the morning of September 11, Ed's aide was on a different floor getting breakfast when the plane crashed into the tower.

Avremel came to Ed's side, and they made their way to a stairwell. Ed's aide was able to return, but it was difficult for her to breathe, so Avremel said he would wait with Ed until several rescue workers would be available to carry him down, and that she could go on without them. As was the case for many that day, both men lost their lives.[5] What a true illustration of friendship and loyalty—of those who stick close to us in times of great need, because they *want* to.

Then there's the fear of failure. I mean, who wants to fail? Who wants to be called a loser? We've all probably heard that old adage, "Winning isn't everything—it's the only thing." I actually had a coach who lived and died by that philosophy. I'm confident we all know that failure is a part of life, but no one actually enjoys experiencing it. Yet, as Teddy Roosevelt once said, "Far better it is to dare mighty things . . . even though checkered by failure . . . than to . . . live in the gray twilight that knows not victory nor defeat."[6]

How about the fear of finance? Perhaps you have told yourself, "I can't afford to go back to school—I have a family"; or, "I can't afford it—I'm a single parent." Remember, we have to quit obsessing about what we cannot do and start believing in what God can do.

By the way, I find it interesting, especially when it comes to financial concerns, that so many people pray for blessings *from* God, but don't want to be a blessing *for* God. Jesus said, "Give to others, and God will give to you" (Luke 6:38 GNT). Notice how God first calls us to obedience. Think about it—why would God give us another loan when we don't even pay on the one we already have?

Finally, sometimes our fear results from lack of faith. I contend that our faith has been built more on the premise of *what if* rather than *he can*. You may have questioned, "What if I step out and it's not what God wants? How do I know it's his will?" God is happier when we take a wrong step with a right heart than if we take no step at all.

FEAR CAN BE FACED

What's the bottom line to all of this? Well, fear is a monster. Fear plays more of a factor in our lives than we sometimes care to admit. If you pull back all the layers of complacency and unfulfilled living, you'll find fear every time. But even though *fear* is inevitable, *misery* is always optional. So, how do we overcome our fears? Let's look in Matthew's gospel where we find the action steps to living our fullest life—the keys to living with no regret and loving without remorse:

> After sending them home, [Jesus] went up into the hills by himself to pray. Night fell while he was there alone. Meanwhile, the disciples were in trouble far away from land,

for a strong wind had risen, and they were fighting heavy waves. About three o'clock in the morning Jesus came toward them, walking on the water. When the disciples saw him walking on the water, they were terrified. In their fear, they cried out, "It's a ghost!" But Jesus spoke to them at once. "Don't be afraid," he said. "Take courage. I am here!" Then Peter called to him, "Lord, if it's really you, tell me to come to you, walking on water." "Yes, come," Jesus said. So Peter went over the side of the boat and walked on the water toward Jesus. (Matt. 14:23–29 NLT)

Step one is to face your fear. Amelia Earhart, the legendary aviator, once said, "The most difficult thing is the decision to act. The rest is merely tenacity. The fears are paper tigers. You can do anything you decide to do."[7] If we're going to live the lives that God intended, and live out our dreams the way God has so perfectly purposed and planned, then we have to step up and look our fears directly in the eye.

Zig Ziglar gave fear two meanings, or acronyms: "Forget Everything and Run or Face Everything and Rise."[8] Facing fear is easier said than done, right? Two things will help: First, expose your fears. Call them out. Identify them. Get those fears "buck naked" so they are completely raw to you and everyone around you. Look at this way: It's like turning on a light in a pitch-black room. Once the light is on, you can see them as they really are. And, ironically, they're probably not as big as you thought. You see, when we expose our fears, we actually minimize their power to paralyze us.

Do you remember the difficulty of going to bed when you were a child? There's just something about the dark, isn't there? Unknown sounds in the dark scare us. Our imaginations run wild. But as soon as a loved one came into the room and turned on the light, things were not as we thought. The same is true with our fears—it's like taking a pair of handcuffs off our wrists. We find freedom to move forward and really live.

Second, we need to express our fears to one another. In today's world, we're not taught to admit our struggles; rather, we're taught to neglect them. By admitting our fears, we not only take responsibility for them, we invite others to walk alongside us so we don't have to face our fears alone. This is exactly why the Bible says, "Two are better than one" (Eccl. 4:9).

FEAR CAN BE REPLACED

Overcoming fear requires you to first step up and face your fear, and then step out and replace your fear with something constructive. That "something constructive" begins with focusing on Christ. Think back to the passage in Matthew. The only way you'll ever walk on water is by first getting out of the boat. I love the fact that Peter's love for Jesus was greater than his fear. Peter knew that Jesus wasn't in the boat; he was on the water. And it's precisely on the water where Jesus invites us to come and trust him.

When we step out and replace our fears, we do need to be aware that our fears may reappear. As the story in Matthew continues, it reads, "When [Peter] noticed the strong wind, he was afraid and started to sink down in the water. 'Save me, Lord!' he cried" (Matt. 14:30 GNT).

You see, it's not necessarily that we will forever conquer our fears; rather, that we contest them in the power of the Holy Spirit. We oppose them in order to witness the greatness of God. Paul wrote to Timothy, "For God has not given us a spirit of fear . . . but of power" (2 Tim. 1:7 NLT). A fear that, at first, is a crippling emotion, now becomes a more ordinary challenge to overcome. Every time we face our fears, our faith is prompted to grow.

I've always been fascinated with skydiving. I imagined the adrenaline rush that would occur the moment before jumping out of a plane. I longed to know what it felt like to just fall from the sky uninhibited. It's something that I always wanted to experience. Finally, a few years ago, I had the privilege of fulfilling that dream. As excited as I was, the fear was very present and very real. I had to decide whether or not that fear was going to keep me from completing my mission. Ultimately, I chose to rise above the fear and jump out of that plane. The view was spectacular—falling from the sky and looking down at God's creation below just made me more in awe of him. That experience is truly something I'll never forget.

Stepping out and replacing your fears means you might fail in the process. That's OK—all successes began with an attempt, but you will fail 100 percent of the time if you never try. "Failure is not an option" should be reworded to, "Failure is an option; quitting is not." Dale Carnegie once said, "Most of the important things in the world have been accomplished by people who have kept on trying when there seemed to be no hope at all."[9]

Peter almost drowned, but his failure also gave him the bragging rights of being the only one other than Jesus to ever walk on water. The fear of failure can sweep over us like a crashing wave; the key is to keep our eyes fixed on Christ. Trust God and see what he can do through your circumstances.

Finally, there may be costs to stepping out and replacing your fears. I'm not talking just about monetary costs. You may experience pain. You could encounter more problems. Your family might think you're nuts. Your friends might leave you high and dry. Replacing your fears may cost time, money, and even your reputation. But remember: every risk that honors God results in reward— though that reward may be unexpected, such as increased courage or wisdom.

I love the story about a man who went out and bought a fifty-thousand-dollar life insurance policy right before he went on a trip. He then went to eat at a Chinese restaurant. His fortune cookie read, "Your recent investment may pay big dividends."

Every time you step out, you could be stepping into difficulties. Every risk has its share of troubles. But as Hudson Taylor, founder of the China Inland Mission (now OMF International), stated, "God's work done in God's way will never lack God's supplies."[10] Every time you step out for God, he will step up for you. It may not end with the result you thought, but when you put your heart into God's hands it will *never* return void. The Bible promises, "We know that in all things God works for the good of those who love him, who have been called according to his purpose" (Rom. 8:28). This includes both failures and successes.

REFLECT

What fears keep me from fulfilling my dreams?

Who can I express my fears to, so that they can walk alongside me? How will I approach them?

Do I believe God is greater than my fears? Why?

Use Time 5 Wisely

Almost every one of us has a problem with time, but the problem we have with time is not with our clocks. Getting mad at the clock is like getting mad at your bathroom scale—the gadget is not at fault if you don't like what it reads. Time is simply a measurement.

Do you remember the daytime soap opera *Days of Our Lives*? Every episode opened with that ever-memorable picture of sand passing through an hourglass. How easily we can feel that represents our lives—how quickly the days seem to pass us by. The Bible says,

"There is a right time and a right way to do everything, but we know so little!" (Eccl. 8:6 GNT). We've all been allotted the same amount of time—168 hours each week. The question is: How are we using them?

TIME MUST BE MANAGED

How many of you have ever felt like the guy in Isaiah who lamented, "I have used up my strength, but have accomplished nothing" (Isa. 49:4 GNT)? I fear that for some of you, this has become your life verse. It's important to remember that if you don't guard your time, someone else will grab it. So how do we guard our time and make sure we are giving it to the things that matter? First, let's look at three things that God says about time.

God says that when we value time, we actually understand how to use it. Effective time management is a mark of wisdom. Paul's instruction was to make "the best use of [your] time" (Eph. 5:16 ESV). To waste it means we don't get it. Time is our life, so we must learn to treasure it.

Second, God says that when we manage our time, we have time. In other words, people who manage their time well don't rush from here to there exclaiming, "There's just never any time!" Did you know that time management is a spiritual act of stewardship? The Bible tells us that everything we have is from God, and our time is no different; it's one of his greatest gifts. Paul wrote, "Now it is required that those who have been given a trust must prove faithful" (1 Cor. 4:2).

Last, God says that when we don't value time or manage it well, we can still learn to do so. Moses prayed, "Teach us to realize the brevity of life, so that we may grow in wisdom" (Ps. 90:12 NLT). Time management is a skill that we can learn—and a skill we *must* learn if we truly want to live out our God-given purpose.

TIME MUST BE PROTECTED

In Paul's letter to the Ephesians, he provided us with three steps toward guarding our time. Let's look at Paul's words: "So be careful how you live. Don't live like fools, but like those who are wise. Make the most of every opportunity in these evil days. Don't act thoughtlessly, but understand what the Lord wants you to do" (Eph. 5:15–17 NLT).

The first step Paul gave is to examine our life. Socrates said, "The unexamined life is not worth living."[1] Yet when it comes to time, too many people are either ignorant or apathetic, sometimes both. I'm reminded of the guy on the street who was asked, "It's been said that in America, the two biggest problems are ignorance and apathy. What do you think?"

And he replied, "I don't know and I don't care."

Paul advised us to pay close attention to how we live. We are to live like the wise, not like the ignorant. Every one of us needs to regularly examine the use of our time. We can't keep saying, "I just don't know where all my time goes." Time never disappears—it all goes somewhere. The question is, where? We need to figure it out.

Long before Paul wrote his words, Moses prayed, "Teach us to number our days" (Ps. 90:12). The reason for numbering something is because that thing matters. When we realize how little time we have, we'll treat it like the precious resource it is. Moses, in his prayer, was simply instructing us to keep a record, to know where, and how, we are spending our time. If we're truly serious about managing our time, then we have to know where it's going.

The second step Paul gave us for guarding our time is to live for today. Again, "Make the most of every chance you get" (Eph. 5:16 MSG). The only opportunity we ever have is right now. We're not promised tomorrow, next week, or next year—but we have right now, today. Each day given to us is a gift from God—that's why it's called the present. Solomon wrote, "Never boast about tomorrow. You don't know what will happen between now and then" (Prov. 27:1 GNT).

Living for today, making the most of right now, means we don't put off things that should be done. Don't procrastinate. Suppose someone handed you 86,400 dollars each morning along with the following instructions: Spend it on anything you want, in any way you want. However, at the end of each day, whatever money you haven't spent, you will forfeit. I suspect you would make sure you spent it all each and every day.

Well, guess what? You have been given just that. Every day, we have all been given 86,400 seconds to spend on anything we want, in any way we want. If we fail to use them, they're gone. There are no carryover minutes in this plan. We must take advantage of what we've been given. As the old saying goes, "If you snooze, you lose."

I'm sure we've all gotten stuff in the mail that says, "for a limited time only—act now!" We should write that on our bathroom mirrors because most of life is "for a limited time only." To look at it any other way would be taking it for granted.

I heard it said once, "Don't kill time, for it has no resurrection." What's done is done, what's lost is lost—we can't get it back. So don't put things off but learn to say no. Learn to eliminate any and all distractions. Here's a little secret I've learned: When you're about the right things, all the wrong things seem to take care of themselves. In short, when you learn to say yes to what you should do, in many ways you say no to what you shouldn't do.

Have you ever noticed that life is filled with vampires? Now I'm not suggesting they are real, as in flesh, but there are time vampires that just suck time right out of our days. Paul wrote, "'I have the right to do anything'—but not everything is constructive" (1 Cor. 10:23). Do you know what he's saying? Kill those vampires! Drive a stake right through their hearts.

TIME MUST BE ORGANIZED AROUND GOD'S PURPOSES

Let's review Paul's instructions for guarding our time: Examine your life, live for today, and third, discover God's purpose for your life. Paul wrote, "Don't act thoughtlessly, but understand what the Lord wants you to do" (Eph. 5:17 NLT). The way you organize your time is related to discovering God's purpose for your life. I've discovered that people organize their lives in one of three ways.

First, some folks organize in the moment, or better said, organize around those moment-to-moment sort of things. These people tend to deem most things as important and urgent. Usually, such a life is marked by hurry.

Second, some people organize around the unfinished. They make to-do lists, and then start their day with what they didn't check off the day before. This kind of life is usually marked with worry. To say, "I'm going to base my life today on what I didn't get done yesterday" never really allows you to get beyond your past. It's literally impossible, then, to live in the present. Every day is a day of catch-up, which means you will never get to a moment where you can slow down and enjoy life.

The third way in which we can organize our time is to build it around what God designed for our lives—his plan and purposes. Look at it like this: When he is our compass, our calendar naturally follows. Which simply means, before you ever figure out what you're going to do, first figure out where you're going. Assume for a moment that you are going on vacation (your goal). You would naturally back-track and plan out all of the things that needed to take place, and when they needed to occur, in order for you to ultimately get on the plane. It's the concept of beginning with the end in mind. In order to hear God's voice, we must take time to be still and listen. Then, once we've heard, our footsteps will follow.

Allow me to help you understand what I mean by compass. Lady Antebellum is an American country group formed in 2006.

Since then, they have become very popular and in 2013, they released another hit, "Compass." If you haven't heard the song, I encourage you to check it out because the lyrics speak to this. Ultimately, where your compass is pointed, your actions will follow.

Your compass is the most important thing when it comes to your time and the management of it. If you don't get this or know this, you will spend your time chasing other things in hopes of finding it. And the sooner you discover your compass will determine how you mark your calendar.

It's like putting a puzzle together without ever knowing the bigger picture. Your compass is that picture on the box that allows you to put the pieces in their place.

Unfortunately, a lot of people live life like the navy pilot during World War II who was lost over the Pacific Ocean. Here's what he radioed in: "I have absolutely no idea where I'm at, but I'm making great time." However, everybody needs a compass, a purpose to live by, to govern time effectively.

When I talk compass, I'm not talking goals. Lots of people have goals. Your compass is not something you shoot for, it's what you shoot with. Your compass is your time management game changer. I've learned it's better to spend your time on a few things that you can do well, rather than spread yourself too thin doing too many things just OK. So for me, I've boiled it down to three areas in which I give my life: First, my person. Remember Jesus' words: "Love your neighbor as you love yourself" (Matt. 19:19 GNT). The most important person in your life (underneath the umbrella of Christ) should be you! Always remember, a battery can't put out what it doesn't have.

Second, I am a partner and parent. If I fail at being a husband and father, I feel as if I've failed completely. My greatest pulpit is my home. I also believe it's one of my greatest witnesses. Paul said that I am to love my wife as Jesus loved the church (see Eph. 5:25). For those of you who are not married or have children, this still applies—you are a partner in all of your relationships, and those relationships require your full attention.

Finally, I'm a pastor—it is the purpose to which God has called me. God has purposed you as well. Perhaps you are a doctor, an educator, or a stay-at-home parent. In any case, it's important that you never neglect this area and continue to seek God's guidance as to how you may use it to bring glory to him.

Kneeling at an altar before God, I made a covenant to be a faithful and good steward of these three areas. God would have never given me a purpose without also giving me all the time and guidance I need to get it done.

Consider for a moment the act of juggling three balls. Anybody can do it; we even teach children to do it. With a little practice and some patience, it is possible. The problems begin when we try to add a fourth ball. The people who can easily juggle four balls are those we find in the circus—we pay to see them!

I contend the same is true with our time and how we juggle it. All too often, people attempt the impossible. Doing more than three things, and thinking you can do them all well, is just plain arrogant—you will end up paying a high price in the end. Time means a great deal to me, and it should to you as well. "Lord, remind me how brief my time on earth will be. Remind me that my days are numbered—how fleeting my life is" (Ps. 39:4 NLT).

REFLECT

Do I often procrastinate? In what ways can I be a better steward of the time God has given me?

What things do I need to say no to in order to guard my time?

Do I organize my time in the moment, around what I didn't finish yesterday, or around God's plan? What changes do I need to make?

Lighten Up... Your Schedules 6

In his book *How Can It Be All Right When Everything Is All Wrong?*, author Lewis Smedes said,

> I bought a brand-new date book recently, the kind I use every year—spiral-bound, black imitation leather covers wrapped around pages and pages of blank squares. Each square has a number to tell me which day of the month I am in at the moment. Each square is a frame for one episode of my life. Before I am through with the book,

I will fill the squares with classes I will teach, people I will eat lunch with, and everlasting committee meetings I will sit through. And these are only the things I cannot afford to forget; I fill the squares, too, with things I do not write down for me to remember, thousands of cups of coffee, some lovemaking, some praying, and, I hope, gestures of help to my neighbors. Whatever I do, it has to fit inside one of those squares on my date book. I live one square at a time. The four lines that make the square are the walls of time that organize my life. Each square has an invisible door that leads to the next square. At a silent stroke, the door opens and I am pulled through it as if by a magnet, sucked into the next square in the line. There I will again fill the time frame that seals me, fill it with my busyness, just as I did the square before. As I get older, the squares seem to get smaller. One day, I will walk into a square that has no door. There will be no mysterious opening and no walking into an adjoining square. One of the squares will be terminal. I do not know which square it will be.[1]

What a graphic picture of what could be the story of our lives. We've made our lives a calendar with little squares all over it, then proceeded with filling them in. Of course, each square is not large enough to fit everything in, is it? We often complain about not having enough hours in a day. We sacrifice our sleep in order to meet demands. We often get to the end of the day wondering where all our time went. This all sounds pretty hopeless, doesn't it? Fear not, there is hope! Let's look at three changes we all can make to help us better manage our busting-at-the-seams schedules.

PRIORITIZE, PRIORITIZE, PRIORITIZE

First, line up your priorities. Proverbs says, "An intelligent person aims at wise action, but a fool starts off in many directions" (Prov. 17:24 GNT). If you have too many irons in the fire, you will actually smother the flame and the fire will burn itself out. The Bible tells us, "It is stupid to waste time on useless projects" (Prov. 12:11 GNT). Look at it this way, it's not that some things are necessarily wrong; they're just not necessary.

What are the priorities in your life? List them. Then look at how you spend your time. If you say your spouse is a priority, do you go on regular dates? If your children are a priority, do you go to their games and concerts or do you often work late instead? Do you spend more time messaging your Facebook friends than you do sitting down face-to-face with them? Does God believe he is a priority in your life—do you regularly give time to him by attending services and spending time in his Word?

It's all about selection. You have to decide what is really important. You'll either live by priority or you'll die underneath the pressure of it all. Corrie ten Boom once said, "If the devil cannot make us bad, he will make us busy."[2] Either way, we miss out on the life God intended for us. So minimize your activities if you want to maximize your potential. You've got to line up your priorities.

LEARN TO LAUGH

The second key is that you have to lighten up—don't take life so seriously. Proverbs says, "Anxiety in a man's heart weighs him down" (Prov. 12:25 ESV). I've heard people say, "You just don't know the amount of stress I'm under."

My question back to them is, "What are you doing under it?"

The American Institute of Stress reported that "stress in the workplace affects four out of five American workers and costs U.S. businesses an estimated $300 billion a year."[3] That's crazy! If we want the stock market to go back up, we've got to get our stress to go back down. The Bible says, "Who of you by worrying [or running around, being busy, or drinking more coffee] can add a single hour to your life?" (Luke 12:25). The answer is nobody.

So let me give you just one simple antidote: Try laughing a little this week. Laughter is an instant stress buster, with both short-term and long-term benefits to the body. The Bible says that stress is not circumstantial, it's an attitude. So don't wait to feel your way into an action, start acting your way into a feeling. Change your attitude—and laugh a little more. "A joyful heart is like good medicine" (Prov. 17:22 ESV).

Humor is one of life's great shock absorbers. Have you ever heard someone say (or maybe said yourself), "Someday we'll all look back on this and laugh"? Here's a thought: Why wait? Need another reason to laugh? Studies tells us that people who laugh are actually more productive than those who don't.[4] I would never suggest that we simply laugh our troubles away. The reality is that it's important at times to face the mountains in our lives, but laughter sure makes those climbs a whole lot easier.

I heard about a businessman who was late for a meeting. He had driven around the block so many times looking for a parking spot that he decided to pull over into a red zone and leave the following note: "This is an absolute emergency. I promise—guarantee—I'll be back in fifteen minutes." He ran up the stairs, made his presentation, and actually returned in only twelve minutes. Much to his dismay, he discovered a ticket on his window. He also found his original note still there, and written in the lower, left corner by the officer: "Take your time." If you were the businessman, would you have laughed at the witty comment by the officer, or would you have let it ruin your afternoon?

Have you ever noticed that things don't always go as planned? At least not in my life. So why is it that we get so easily worked up when we need to shift things around a bit? Permit me to offer a couple "rules of engagement" for dealing with such moments: First, never sweat the small stuff; and second, it's usually all small stuff. Actually it's always small stuff when compared to the greatness of God.

SEEK GOD

The last key to managing your schedule is to always look up. If I were to survey a hundred people and ask what keeps them from knowing and loving God more, I'm confident that the top answer would be, "I'm just too busy." Here's the irony—the early followers of Christ couldn't be stopped by persecution, poverty, imprisonment, or martyrdom, but we can be easily stunted by something as trivial as too much on our to-do lists.

Our problem is never horizontal, as in our relationships with each other; our problem is vertical, in our relationship with God. The early church didn't advance because they condensed worship, prayer, serving, and hanging out with each other. It flourished because of their unbelievable commitment to those things—to looking up.

Maybe you think, "If I could just get a little more time." You don't need a little more time; you need a lot more God. The Bible tells us that "Fear of the LORD lengthens one's life" (Prov. 10:27 NLT). H. Jackson Brown Jr. said, "Don't say you don't have enough time. You have exactly the same number of hours per day that were given to Helen Keller, Pasteur, Michaelangelo, Mother Teresa, Leonardo da Vinci, Thomas Jefferson, and Albert Einstein."[5]

God has given us all the time we need to accomplish the things that he purposed and planned. So look up, not around. It's not about doing the things that lie around us, but about walking in step with the One who lies within us.

Do you know what *reverence* means? It means taking God seriously. One of the great illusions of our day is that we call ourselves Christians but we don't truly follow Christ—our walk isn't matching our talk. And then we wonder why our lives seem so out of control. When we improve the vertical, the horizontal will naturally fall into place. Remember, we emulate what we spend time around. "Trust the LORD with all your heart. . . . Seek his will in all you do, and he will show you which path to take" (Prov. 3:5–6 NLT).

Now here's a man who understands the vertical. Robert Murray M'Cheyne said the following:

> I ought to pray before seeing any one. Often when I sleep long, or meet with others early, it is eleven or twelve o'clock before I begin secret prayer. This is a wretched system. It is unscriptural. Christ arose before day and went into a solitary place. David says: "Early will I seek thee"; "Thou shalt early hear my voice." Family prayer loses much of its power and sweetness, and I can do no good to those who come to seek from me. The conscience feels guilty, the soul unfed, the lamp not trimmed. Then when in secret prayer the soul is often out of tune, I feel it is far better to begin with God—to see his face first, to get my soul near him before it is near another.[6]

If Christ is to be our example, shouldn't we also follow his example in our prayer lives? Several verses throughout the Gospels illustrate the fact that he made it a priority to stay connected to the vine—his Father. The Bible tells us to "seek first *his* kingdom" (Matt. 6:33, emphasis added). How else do you seek if you're not regularly in prayer?

Jesus posed a question that we need to answer (better now than later): "What can anyone give in exchange for their soul?" (Mark 8:37). Every day we exchange our lives for something. The question is, what are we exchanging it for? Are you looking up and giving your best to him? Are you giving your minimum to the mediocre?

If you feel your schedule is out of control, the schedule isn't the problem—you are. When your time is under your control, your life will be less out of control. Master your time and you master your life.

We need an administrator who truly understands us better than we understand ourselves. May I recommend someone? Jesus said, "Come to me, all you who are weary and burdened, and I will give you rest" (Matt. 11:28). That's the best deal I've ever heard.

REFLECT

What does my schedule look like? In what ways do I need to prioritize better?

Can I easily step back and laugh, or do I let stress and anger get the better of me? What changes do I need to make?

Do I continuously look up, or do I look around? How can I improve my prayer life?

Don't Waste 7 Your Mind

One of the great robbers that inhibits us from achieving our God-given dreams is our minds. The Bible tells us that we are to prepare our minds for action; and be sober-minded (see 1 Pet. 1:13 ESV). The word *prepare* in the Greek language literally means "to gird up"—like a soldier who would cinch up his belt. Our minds are a very special gift, and we need to use this gift to its fullest.

FILTER YOUR MIND

So how do we do this? How do we protect our minds? Let me give you two simple steps: The first is, filter it. You know the old saying, "Garbage in, garbage out." We have to choose, because if we don't, whatever we allow into our minds will one day come out in our lives. The Bible tells us to "take captive every thought to make it obedient to Christ" (2 Cor. 10:5).

I did a little research on home security systems. Every company requires a monthly fee and an initial set-up fee. But the features! One company's system includes a keypad, three sensors, a motion detector light, an interior siren, a control panel, a yard sign, and window decals (you've got to love the decals—I know that was the selling point for me). What's my point? We'll go a long way to protect our stuff.

I know this firsthand because my wife and I are experts on break-ins. I'm not kidding—our home has been broken into four times! Our neighbors love us but we're a magnet for crooks. Did I mention the police know us on a first-name basis? Needless to say, we now have a home security system because our stuff matters.

But how much more important are our minds than our stuff? And yet, we invest more time and effort into protecting our possessions than we do our minds. This needs to change. Here's a thought: If you take my things and I still have my mind, I can get more things. But if you take my mind and leave my stuff, it doesn't really matter because I now lack the mental capacity to use what I still have.

God gave us one of the biggest security systems for our minds and it's free—no monthly payments! It's our eyes. The Bible says: "The eye is the lamp of the body. If your eyes are healthy, your whole body will be full of light" (Matt. 6:22). We need to monitor what we watch.

Did you know that Americans have their televisions on almost seven hours every day—which equates to almost twenty-five hundred hours of TV each year? And if you live to be sixty-five, you would amass over eighteen years of solid television viewing. That's not amazing. It's outrageous! And 49 percent of Americans even admit to watching too much TV.[1] Worse still is that if we went to church every Sunday and never missed a weekend, and we lived to be sixty-five, it would equate to almost five months. Now that's sad.

David wrote, "I will refuse to look at anything vile and vulgar" (Ps. 101:3 NLT). That's the filter I'm talking about. David made a promise to himself, as well as to God, that he wasn't going to look at anything that could bring about harm or be unhealthy. We need to make the same commitment. In short, monitor what you watch. Again, Jesus said that our eyes are the lamp of our bodies, and if our eyes are good, our whole bodies will be full of light. But if our eyes are bad, our bodies will be "full of darkness" (Luke 11:34).

Here are a few things you can do to transform your eyes into that ever-necessary security system. Drop cable television for a while (maybe forever). Be careful with the movies you watch and the Internet. There are incredible filters you can place on your computer. Again, it's important to have a mind filter.

FEED YOUR MIND

The second step to protecting your mind is to feed it with the right things. When you protect your mind from certain things, it's important to then feed it with the right stuff. The Bible says, "Fix your thoughts on what is true, and honorable, and right, and pure. . . . Think about things that are excellent and worthy of praise" (Phil. 4:8 NLT). Solomon wrote, "Wise men and women are always learning" (Prov. 18:15 MSG). Nature abhors a vacuum: If you want to keep the bad things out, it's vital that you put the right things in. Being a Christian means we are committed to a lifelong process of learning. The word *disciple* literally means "a learner." Therefore, if we are not learning, we are not being Jesus' disciple.

By the time we reach our forties our cognitive abilities generally begin to decline.[2] The way we combat this decline is to continue learning. Ask yourself when the last time was that you learned or acquired a new skill, a new truth, a new thought, or a new attitude. You see, if we're going to protect our minds, then we have to keep feeding them. We need to always be learning and longing for mental food.

Facilitate the Feeding

I contend that in order to feed our minds, we must develop three attitudes that facilitate the process: First, be open. "Intelligent people are always ready to learn. Their ears are open for knowledge" (Prov. 18:15 NLT). Openness says, "I can learn from anybody, any place, at any time."

Second, be humble. This attitude says, "I don't know everything." And the reality is, no one does. Solomon wrote, "When pride comes, then comes disgrace, but with humility comes wisdom" (Prov. 11:2).

Third, be eager. We learn faster when we're excited about something. "An intelligent person is always eager to take in more truth" (Prov. 15:14 MSG). If we're going to feed our minds, then we must wake up every day and pray, "Lord, teach me something new today. Help me to be mentally alert. I'm open, humble, and eager to learn."

Feeding Requires Action

Now, with that all said, let me give you three simple, yet practical, ways we can feed our minds: First, schedule think time. I believe that a lot of people don't spend enough time thinking today. We've become a nation of zombies; we don't think—we just act. Somebody once said that 5 percent of the world truly thinks, 10 percent thinks they think, and 85 percent would rather die than think (or at least prefer to have someone else do their thinking for them).[3]

One of the great gifts God gave us is this ability to think. Imagine how different our lives would be if we'd just slow down and start thinking things through. We have to engage our brains. While this can be easier said than done, especially in a world that is running faster than our thoughts, we must be intentional about following Paul's advice: "Make it your ambition to lead a quiet life" (1 Thess. 4:11).

Second, schedule reading time. It's been said that if you are not reading, you are not feeding. When was the last time you read a good book? When was the last time you visited a library? When was the last time you read the Bible? Believe it or not, you can actually read yourself out of a rut. So start reading more. By the way, did you know that Americans spend more money on beer than books?[4] Perhaps that's why our stomachs are larger than our brains. If you're not reading, I contend that you're not growing. And if you're not growing, what in the world are you giving?

Third and last, schedule time with wise people. "Walk with the wise and become wise" (Prov. 13:20 NLT). There's amazing power in association. You can't fly with the eagles if you're going to run with the turkeys. You become like those you hang around. The Bible tells us, "Blessed is the one who does not walk in step with the wicked or stand in the way that sinners take or sit in the company of mockers" (Ps. 1:1).

It's a commonly held understanding that we are what we eat. Translate that to we become what we think. When God gave us a mind, he gave us an incredible gift, and it's our responsibility to use it, develop it, and keep it sharp. Imagine the life we can live when we choose to feed, fuel, and fund our minds with good, healthy, godly stuff.

REFLECT

What specific mind filters do I need to put in place?

In what ways am I currently feeding my mind? In what ways should I be feeding it?

Am I humble and do I seek to glean from those around me who are wise? In what ways?

Treasure 8
Your Body

The people of North America make up just 6 percent of the entire world's population; however, we account for a whopping 34 percent of the world's weight. Compare that with Asia, which contributes 61 percent to the world's population, yet claims only 13 percent of the weight.[1] Our health is obviously a major concern in today's world. In fact, when Yankee Stadium in New York City was rebuilt in 2009, they installed wider seats, thereby reducing overall capacity by over four thousand seats.[2] Houston, we have a problem! The apostle John wrote, "I pray that you may enjoy good health and that all may go well with you, even as your soul is getting along well" (3 John 1:2). People are overweight and out of shape.

I'm not intending to be critical or judgmental, but we all know that *how we act* has a great deal to do with *how we feel*. God desires for us to be healthy. The Bible says that you are to "honor God with your body" (1 Cor. 6:20 NLT). If we're going to experience God's purpose for our lives, then one of the areas we need to take seriously is our health.

RESPECT YOUR BODY

Here are three keys to taking back your physical body for God's spiritual good: First, you must learn to respect it. What crosses your mind when you think about your body? Some reject it—they simply hate their bodies. Another group of people seek to perfect it—they go as far as plastic surgery or become addicted to working out. Others just neglect their bodies—they become couch potatoes. But there is one more response, and I believe it's the right attitude—the God attitude—and that is to respect it. Respecting our bodies means that we (1) choose to be OK with the bodies God gave us, and (2) that we take care of our bodies to the best of our abilities.

"What [a man] thinks is what he really is" (Prov. 23:7 GNT). If we're going to experience good health, then we have to change our attitude toward our own bodies. The Bible instructs, "Learn to appreciate and give dignity to your body, not abusing it, as is so common among those who know nothing of God" (1 Thess. 4:4–5 MSG).

PROTECT YOUR BODY

This brings me to the second key to taking back our bodies, and that's learning to protect them. Why? Well first, we'll feel better physically. It's a fact. Exercise gives us more energy. We think better, and our reaction to everyday irritations is with a calmer demeanor since exercise is a natural stress reliever. I've heard it said that health is what makes today feel like the best day of your life.

Protecting our bodies allows our confidence to grow. When you feel like you look better, you just start acting better. Good health fuels a desire for something better.

Finally, if we protect our bodies we live longer. Now, I understand there's no guarantee, but countless studies support this idea.

Personally, I want to protect my body for three vital reasons. First, because God made it. The Bible says that God created us in our mother's womb and that we are "fearfully and wonderfully made" (Ps. 139:14). When was the last time you said to yourself that you are fearfully and wonderfully made by God?

Several years ago, I had the privilege of driving a BMW Z3 roadster. If you're not familiar with this car, I have to tell you—it's just incredible! They are handmade works of art and not easy to come by. Driving the Z3 was a once-in-a-lifetime opportunity, and I took it. The power in this vehicle is like no other. It was an extraordinary drive. The craftsmanship is outstanding. A lot of thought and work went into making this car what it is today (and that has a great deal to do with why it costs so much as well). But as great as that roadster was, I can't help but realize how much greater we are. We, too, have been handcrafted, perfectly designed and created by God. And when he saw us, he said, "it was very good" (Gen. 1:31).

Second, I want to protect my body because God paid for it. Check out the price tag on the Z3 and then imagine how much more we're worth in God's eyes. Notice what Paul wrote to the church in Corinth: "You do not belong to yourself, for God bought you with a high price. So you must honor God with your body" (1 Cor. 6:19–20 NLT). That's incredible! Our bodies are not only a gift, but we were bought by God himself.

Finally, God lives in my body. "Surely you know that you are God's temple and that God's Spirit lives in you!" (1 Cor. 3:16 GNT). Understand that a temple is not an object to be worshiped; it's a place designed for worship—the place in which God resides. So why not take care of your body and prepare it as a place for worship to God?

DIRECT YOUR BODY

Let's review the keys to taking back our physical bodies for God's spiritual good. First, we must learn to respect our bodies. Second, we need to learn to protect our bodies. Finally, we need to direct our bodies—point them toward God's principles and design. "Pay attention to what I say; turn your ear to my words. . . . For they are life . . . and health to one's whole body" (Prov. 4:20–22). There are many diets that we can subscribe to, but there is nothing like God's health plan. The principles in his Word are not just there for our spiritual good, they exist for our emotional and physical well-being, too.

Let me help you with this. If we are going to direct our bodies, we need to *eat to live* rather than *live to eat*. Some of you have been on a balanced diet for far too long. Not the balanced diet that you read about in the health magazines—your idea of a balanced diet is having a hamburger in both hands. It's time to change your eating habits. We need to get off the fast food lifestyle and start living for God's faith foods—which have eternal weight.

"You know the old saying, 'First you eat to live, and then you live to eat'? Well, it may be true that the body is only a temporary thing, but that's no excuse for stuffing your body with food. . . . Since the Master honors you with a body, honor him with your body!" (1 Cor. 6:13 MSG). I invite you to change your perception of who you are in Christ. Stop seeing yourself as a body with a soul, and start seeing yourself as a soul with a body. Trust me—that alone can help considerably.

Work out rather than eat out. I'm told you know when you're out of shape when you feel like "the morning after" but you didn't go out the night before, or when your knees buckle and your belt won't. One guy described himself by saying, "I'm not overweight; I just need to be six inches taller."

Many believe in the benefits of exercise; they just don't know how to commit to it. Theodore Roosevelt wrote, "The human body has two ends on it: one to create with and one to sit on. Sometimes people get their ends reversed."[3]

Permit me to offer a new diet. It's called the past-da diet. Here's how it works: You walk past-da pie, past-da doughnuts, and past-da ice cream. Actually, one of the simplest, and best, exercise programs I've ever heard of was actually told to me by one of my staff: "Just push away from the table." You will win on two accounts—the weight goes down and your biceps will actually bulk up.

Go to sleep rather than sleep to go. Friends, there's a big difference between rest and sleep. The Bible says, "God gives rest to his loved ones" (Ps. 127:2 NLT). Let me ask you something: when does your day begin—five or six in the morning? According to the Bible, God started each day in the evening. Genesis uses the phrase "and there was evening, and there was morning" to describe each of the six days of creation. This indicates to us that the twenty-four-hour cycle we know as "a day" actually begins in the evening—the same reason that the Jewish Sabbath is observed from sundown to sundown. Isn't that interesting? Our day is not to begin when we get up, but rather when we go to sleep.

Throughout the night, several ninety-minute sleep cycles occur. Each cycle contains both non-REM (ranging from light to deep sleep) and REM (where dreams often occur) sleep. It is during non-REM deep sleep that our bodies are able to restore themselves. Interestingly, this non-REM deep sleep occurs in a higher proportion between the hours of 11:00 p.m. and 3:00 a.m. Between 3:00 and 7:00 a.m., this restorative deep sleep decreases, and REM (dreaming) sleep increases.[4] What does all this mean? If we don't go to bed at a reasonable time each night, we will miss our opportunity to receive our deepest, restorative rest. Our bodies are gifts designed by God. Thus, we ought to treat them like the temples they are and allow healing time from the daily stresses we face.

Let me leave you with a fun thought: If you sleepwalk, you can actually get your rest and exercise at the same time. Now, that's pretty cool!

REFLECT

Do I truly respect my body as a gift given by God and as a temple in which he resides? Why or why not?

Am I directing my body toward God's principles and design? What does that look like?

What changes do I need to make to my eating, sleeping, and exercising habits?

Choose Your 9 Friends Wisely

Loneliness was never a part of God's plan. From our very inception, God created us for relationships—a relationship with him, and relationships with others. "The LORD God said, 'It is not good for the man to be alone'" (Gen. 2:18). In fact, without relationships, there is no living—only existing. Solomon wrote, "Two are better than one" (Eccl. 4:9).

It's imperative that we don't seek just any old relationships, but God-centered, God-focused relationships. "Do not be misled: 'Bad company corrupts good character'" (1 Cor. 15:33). If we're going to live out our God-purposed dreams for our lives, then we need to develop healthy, God-fearing relationships. The Bible says, "The righteous choose their friends carefully" (Prov. 12:26).

IRON SHARPENS IRON

How do we find and foster these relationships? First, get friends who make you think. "As iron sharpens iron, so a friend sharpens a friend" (Prov. 27:17 NLT). There's a lot of talk about being formed into Christ's image, but from my vantage point, it's pretty much just that—talk. Be honest: Do you really want to be formed into the image of Christ? If your answer is yes, then it's essential to have some hammers and anvils in your life. I'm not suggesting surrounding yourself with self-righteous, mean people, but instead with those who truly care about your eternal future and soul. You see, a lot of people will say they want Christ to change them, but they don't want to go through the pain of getting pounded and formed into Christ's image—they want easy relationships. We all have blind spots in our lives, and we need the kind of friends who will point them out to us. "Faithful are the wounds of a friend" (Prov. 27:6 ESV). We all need people who will sharpen us. As Ralph Waldo Emerson said, "Make us do what we can."[1]

This is exactly what my friends do for me—they make me think. The Bible says that one of the main reasons for friends is to stimulate us, motivate us, and challenge us. Great friends—true friends—make you think. Remember, we're all diamonds in the rough—diamonds that require chipping and refining.

FRIENDS FOR THE LONG HAUL

Second, we all need friends who really care. The Bible says, "A friend loves at *all* times" (Prov. 17:17 ESV, emphasis added). I'm tired of people who call me a friend, but as soon as sparks fly, so do they. True friends don't do that. True friends care more about the relationship than they do about their own feelings. I heard it said that a true friend is still standing with you when everyone else is gone.

Friends who really care will be unquestionably honest. I don't know about you, but I need honesty, not flattery. Flattery is nice sometimes, but I want friends who will let me know when I have a "hanger" (a booger that is hanging out of your nose).

My friends tell me what I need to hear not what I want to hear—and there's a big difference. Sometimes the truth hurts, doesn't it? It's like a surgeon's scalpel—it has to cut before healing can take place. The fact is, sometimes we all need to be cut open and fully exposed. But after surgery, my friends are still there for the recovery. I want people who care enough to tell me when I'm blowing it. I want people who care enough to tell me when I'm making a mistake. A true friend will always take that risk.

Friends who really care will be undeniably dependable. In essence, you can *always* count on them. The Bible tells us that a friend never abandons a friend (see Prov. 27:10). Did you know that a synonym for *friendship* is *loyalty*? It's like playing with super glue—you just can't get rid of them. (Of course, who would want to?)

During World War II, there were two buddies who were inseparable. They enlisted together, trained together, and fought together. During an attack, one of them was critically wounded and unable to crawl back to the bunker. It would be suicidal for the other to try to reach him, yet his friend decided to try anyway. Before he could get out of the bunker, his sergeant ordered him not to go. "It's too late," the sergeant barked. "You'll do him no good, and you'll get yourself killed."

A few minutes later, when his sergeant turned his back, he slipped out the door. As he staggered back, now fatally wounded himself, with his friend dead in his arms, his sergeant blurted, "What a waste. He's dead and you're dying. It just wasn't worth it."

With his last breath, the dying man replied, "Oh, yes it was, Sarge. When I got to him, the only thing he said was, 'I knew you'd come.'"[2]

That's what friends do. "The greatest love you can show is to give your life for your friends" (John 15:13 GNT).

Years ago a friend told me, "I'll be your best friend or your worst nightmare, you choose. But either way, I'm not going anywhere." He stuck to his word; he hasn't gone anywhere, and for that I'm forever grateful.

Friends who really care will be unconditionally accepting. They will love you no matter what. Have you ever wondered about the life of a frog? They're low and slow, ugly and puffy, pooped and drooped. The frog feeling comes when you want to be bright, but you feel dumb. When you want to share, but would rather be selfish. When you want to be thankful, but feel resentful. When you want to be great, but see yourself as ever so small. When you want to care, but remain indifferent. At one time or another, I'm sure we have all found ourselves on a lily pad, floating down the great river of life—frightened, lonely, hurting, and too froggish to budge.

The Brothers Grimm classic fairy tale collection included an early version of this story: Once upon a time there was a frog. Only he wasn't really a frog, he was a prince who looked and felt like a frog. A wicked witch had cast a spell on him, and the only thing that could save him was a kiss from a beautiful maiden. But cute chicks typically don't go around kissing frogs, do they? So he just sat there, an unkissed prince in a frog suit. That is, until one day when a beautiful maiden gathered him up and gave him a big old smack. Poof! There he was, a frog-turned-handsome prince, and they lived happily ever after.[3]

You know the story. The point is that we need to start kissing frogs, right? To be accepting, yes, but there is another perspective. If you're the frog, you need to hang around people who will truly accept you. Acceptance means being valued *all* the time. It means you're not forced into someone else's ideas of who you should be. It means your ideas are taken seriously. It means you can talk about how you feel and why you feel a certain way—because those feelings matter. It means you're safe to be you, and no one is going to destroy you out of their own prejudices. I have a friend who says, "You're a good old egg, even though you're a little cracked."

TRUE FELLOWSHIP

Get friends who make you think. Get friends who really care. And finally, get friends who are committed to helping you grow in Christ. We can all be friends with people who don't follow Christ, but *true* fellowship requires that we're going in the same direction. My friends are first and foremost committed to my eternal future. The Bible tells us, "Don't become partners with those who reject God. How can you make a partnership out of right and wrong? That's not partnership; that's war. Is light best friends with dark? Does Christ go strolling with the Devil? Do trust and mistrust hold hands?" (2 Cor. 6:14–15 MSG).

Now, I'm not suggesting that we ignore or even isolate ourselves from those who don't know Christ. Quite the contrary—how would they know him if we don't go to them? But what I want you to understand is that when you're around them, never forget whose you are and what they need to become. You are the light in their life—illuminate *them,* not the other way around.

Someone once said that a friend is one who knows you as you are, understands where you've been, accepts who you've become, and still gently invites you to grow.

Let me close this chapter by asking this: Do you want a life of influence, impact, integrity, character, honor, love, purity, legacy, and family? Do you want a life of being beaten down, insecure, selfish, guilty, shamed, abandoned, bitter, angry, and depressed? I have discovered that when you really boil it down, there are only two types of friends—balcony and basement. People will either pull you up or bring you down. Which kind of friend are you, and which ones do you have?

REFLECT

Am I open with my friends? Do I allow them to tell me what I need to hear, not just what I want to hear, or am I immediately defensive? Why?

Am I unconditionally accepting of my friends, or do I tend to walk away if I get hurt? How can I become more open to their loving suggestions?

Do I have friends who help me grow in Christ? Who can I reach out to as I develop these relationships?

Spread 10 the Love

There's nothing more powerful than a focused life—a life that knows where it's going and what it wants to accomplish. Consider light: Diffused, it spreads out and covers more area, which can be beneficial. But focused, it can cut through steel. It's called a laser. That's the power of focus, and the same is true with our lives. Though God desires that we illuminate his love, he also wants us to live focused lives. As the old saying goes, if you aim at nothing, you'll hit it every time. But the moment we focus our lives, we have power.

To quote George Bernard Shaw: "I am of the opinion that my life belongs to the whole community, and as long as I live it is a privilege to do for it whatever I can. I want to be thoroughly used up when I die, for the harder I work the more I live. I rejoice in life for its own sake. Life is no 'brief candle' for me. It is a sort of splendid torch which I have got hold of for the moment, and I want to make it burn as brightly as possible before handing it on to future generations."[1]

In the book of Matthew, Jesus taught us the need for focus. "What a generation! No sense of God! No focus to your lives! How many times do I have to go over these things? How much longer do I have to put up with this?" (Matt. 17:17 MSG). We need to take a lesson from Moses' prayer in Psalm 90 and pray, "God, remind me what's important in life. Help me remember what matters most." In Paul's letter to the church of Philippi, we can see evidence of his focused life: "Not that I have already obtained all this, or have already arrived at my goal, but I press on to take hold of that for which Christ Jesus took hold of me. Brothers and sisters, I do not consider myself yet to have taken hold of it. But one thing I do: Forgetting what is behind and straining toward what is ahead, I press on toward the goal to win the prize for which God has called me heavenward in Christ Jesus" (Phil. 3:12–14).

Too often, our past imprisons us. Yet we'd rather stay there than press on beyond it. But if we're going to experience and exercise the power of God, we must press on, become like a laser, and not allow the things of this world to sidetrack us.

I don't know what God desires for you specifically. However, I can provide you with three nonnegotiable life objectives that, when implemented, can ensure you remain focused in life. By not doing them, you may forfeit God's will for your life.

GIVE YOUR LOVE

First and foremost, the best thing we can do is love. Paul told us that love should be our "highest goal" (1 Cor. 14:1 NLT). He wrote in his first letter to the Corinthians, "No matter what I say, what I believe, and what I do, I'm bankrupt without love" (13:3 MSG). Aren't we all?

One day a guy went to Jesus and asked what life was really all about, and Jesus replied, "Love me and love people" (Mark 12:30–31, author's paraphrase). According to the Bible, that's our beacon to the world identifying us as God's followers: how we "love one another" (John 13:35).

Being a pastor, I have stood at the bedside of people who were dying. Not once have I heard one say, "Bring me my diplomas. I want to look at my portfolio." Without fail, they always want their loved ones beside them.

I witnessed love in action at the opening games for our state's Special Olympics in 2011. I was honored to be on the planning committee and wanted to make sure the event was a hit. The year before, I had attended the opening ceremonies and was devastated to see so few people supporting these athletes. I told myself that wasn't going to happen the next year, so I joined the planning committee. Needless to say, it was nothing short of amazing. I asked my church family to pour out their love on these amazing athletes—and they responded in a big way. The place was absolutely packed—so much so that the fire marshal wasn't too pleased!

I love the prayer that Paul offered for the church in Thessalonica: "May the Lord make your love for one another and for all people grow and overflow" (1 Thess. 3:12 NLT). This is my prayer for you. The best thing we can do—*always*—is love.

GIVE YOUR TIME

The best expression of love is giving of our time. Time is the most precious thing we have, and, too often, we spend it on things that don't really matter. As I stated previously, our days are numbered. We cannot add to them; we have been allotted only so many. Thus, the moment we give someone our time, we actually give them a piece of our life—a piece we cannot get back.

The disciple John said: "Let us not love with words or speech but with action and in truth" (1 John 3:18). If you say you love but you're not giving any time, you're just kidding yourself. Our families and friends don't want our provisions or possessions, they want our person. But if they can't get our person, they'll take our provisions and possessions.

Read these words written by a workaholic father:

I have a son who is five years old, a boy so very fine.
When I look at him, it seems to me that all the world is mine.
But seldom do I ever see my son awake and bright.
I only see him when he sleeps. I'm only home at night.

When I come home so weary in the darkness after day
My wife then says to me, "You should have seen him play."
So I stand beside his bed and I look and ponder there
And I wonder if he's dreaming, "Why isn't Daddy here?"[2]

The statistics regarding absent fathers are staggering. According to *Best Life* magazine, in 2006, "About 40 percent of children living with their mothers have not seen their fathers even once in the last year."[3] That's just wrong! Kids need our love given as time, and huge chunks of it—and that goes for *both* parents. I've often heard it said, and maybe you have as well, that kids don't need quantity time, they need quality time. I'd argue we need to give them both.

DO IT NOW

The best time to love is now. Not yesterday or tomorrow, but right now. My high school teacher used to tell me, "Never put off until tomorrow what you can do today." According to the Bible, today is all we have. Paul wrote, "Whenever we have the opportunity, we should do good to everyone" (Gal. 6:10 NLT).

A lot of things in life can wait, but love can't. Now is the time. Author Chuck Colson wrote, "As I think back on my own life, my biggest regret is not spending more time with my children. Making family your top priority means standing against a culture where materialism and workaholism are rampant. It means realizing that you may not advance as fast in your career as some of your colleagues—at least for a few years. It means being willing to accept a lower standard of living . . . knowing you're doing the right thing for your children, giving them the emotional security they'll draw on for the rest of their lives."[4]

Keep the main thing the main thing. Love. Give someone your time. Let yourself be interrupted. Stay focused on the One who matters and your life will follow. When it's all said and done, it won't be what you accumulated that will matter; it will be who you loved and how much you loved.

Several years ago, I was told that someone in our city placed an online classified ad asking for a Bible. Within hours, seven different people showed up at his door to give him one. The cool thing? All seven people were from the church where I serve as pastor. I love to watch love in action!

REFLECT

Is the power of focus prevalent in my life? Why or why not?

Am I freely giving of my love? In what areas of my life do I need to be more loving?

Am I freely giving of my time? With whom do I need to spend more time with?

Epilogue

God has offered each of us an amazing gift—life! It's a gift that he desires to be full and abundant. It can be all that he purposed it to be, but whether it achieves that abundance depends on a choice we must make. We must choose to stop focusing on what we cannot do and start believing in what God can do through us.

We each have formulated our own dreams, whether on paper or just in our minds. Some of us have already scratched off things we've accomplished; yet others of us have tossed some goals aside simply because we believe they'll never happen. We've given up. Somewhere along the way we started counting minutes instead of embracing moments.

God didn't create us to be like chickens that simply scratch and peck around the yard. He made us to be eagles; he has given us wings to fly in order for us to fully experience life and the moments he grants us. I pray that we would never reduce ourselves and settle for less when he has intended so much more for us. He loves it when we dare to dream the impossible, because the Bible says that what is impossible for man is possible with him.

Our Father created us to truly live a life of no regrets; to truly love without remorse—and it's a choice he has given us to make. I pray that God would move all of us in such a way that we would choose very carefully.

Chapter 1

1. *Finding Nemo*, directed by Andrew Stanton and Lee Unkrich (Burbank, CA: Walt Disney Feature Animation, 2003), DVD.

2. This story is a paraphrased version of Ralph Phelps sermon entitled "How to Worry" found at Bible.org, last updated February 2, 2009, https://bible.org/illustration/matthew-625-34.

3. George Seldes, comp., *The Great Quotations* (New York: Pocket Books, 1978), 611.

Chapter 2

1. Kenneth D. Kochanek, Jiaquan Xu, Sherry L. Murphy, Arialdi M Miniño, and Hsiang-Ching Kung, Division of Vital Statistics, "Deaths: Final Data for 2014," National Vital Statistics Report, June 30, 2016, http://www.cdc.gov/nchs/data/nvsr/nvsr65/nvsr65_04.pdf.

2. Walter D. Wintle, "The Man Who Thinks He Can," in *Poems That Live Forever*, comp. Hazel Felleman (New York: Doubleday, 1965), 310.

3. "Charles Schulz quotes," QuoteCorner.com, accessed November 1, 2012, http://quotecorner.com/Charles-Schulz-quotes.html.

4. Stephen N. Rummage, paraphrased from Mark Twain, soundfaith, last updated in 2008, https://soundfaith.com/sermons/21285-the-greatest-general.

5. "Oscar Wilde quotes," Thinkexist.com, accessed November 1, 2012, http://thinkexist.com/quotation/be_yourself-everyone_else_is_already_taken/341131.html.

6. Steven J. Lawson, *Holman Old Testament Commentary: Job*, ed. Max Anders (Nashville, TN: Broadman and Holman, 2004), 253.

7. Olutosin O. Ogunkolade, *Great Words for Great Living* (Bloomington, IN: AuthorHouse Publishing, 2011), 434.

8. William Safire and Leonard Safir, eds., *Words of Wisdom: More Good Advice* (New York: Simon and Schuster, 1989), 102.

Chapter 3

1. "Man Encounters Lazy Shoe Repair Shop," Preaching Today, accessed October 19, 2016, http://www.preachingtoday.com/illustrations/2008/march/6032408.html.

2. John Ortberg, "Ruthlessly Eliminate Hurry," Christianity Today, accessed November 1, 2012, http://www.christianitytoday.com/le/2002/july-online-only/cln20704.html?start=1.

Chapter 4

1. "Fear," TanBible.com, accessed November 1, 2012, http://www.tanbible.com/tol_ill/fear.htm.

2. "Brush with 'Rattlesnake,'" The Spokesman-Review, accessed October 19, 2016, https://news.google.com/newspapers?nid=1314&dat=19660426&id=FGtWAAAAIBAJ&sjid=D-kDAAAAIBAJ&pg=5597,3515480&hl=en.

3. "Fear," TanBible.com, accessed November 1, 2012, http://www.tanbible.com/tol_ill/fear.htm.

4. Ibid.

5. Yosef Ben Shlomo Hakohen, "Friendship and Loyalty," Aish.com, 2002, accessed November 1, 2012, http://www.aish.com/ci/be/48881527.html.

6. Alex Barnett, ed., *Words That Changed America: Great Speeches That Inspired, Challenged, Healed, and Enlightened* (Guilford, CT: Lyons Press, 2003), 208.

7. "Quotes by Amelia Earhart," Amelia Earhart: The Official Website, accessed November 1, 2012, http://www.ameliaearhart.com/about/quotes.html.

8. "Zig Ziglar quote," Daily Inspirational Quotes, accessed November 1, 2016, http://www.dailyinspirationalquotes.in/2016/04/21/f-e-r-two-meanings-forget-everything-run-face-everything-rise-choice-zig-ziglar/.

9. Jan Karon, *A Continual Feast: Words of Comfort and Celebration, Collected by Father Tim* (New York: Penguin Books, 2006).

10. "Voices of the Past," OMF International, accessed November 1, 2012, https://omf.org/us/about/our%20story/quotes/.

Chapter 5

1. Plato, *The Trial and Death of Socrates*, Trans. G. M. A. Grube, rev. John M. Cooper (Indianapolis, IN: Hackett Publishing Company, Inc., 2000), 39.

Chapter 6

1. Lewis B. Smedes, *How Can It Be All Right When Everything Is All Wrong?* (Colorado Springs, CO: WaterBrook Press, 1999), 179–180.

2. "Corrie ten Boom Quotes," goodreads, accessed November 1, 2016, http://www.goodreads.com/quotes/655841-if-the-devil-cannot-make-us-bad-he-will-make.

3. Lisa Quast, "Summer Is a Good Time to Think about How to Reduce Stress at Work," Forbes, accessed November 1, 2012, http://www.forbes.com/sites/lisaquast/2012/07/30/summer-is-a-good-time-to-think-about-how-to-reduce-stress-at-work/#30d746c97cda.

4. Gwen Parkes, "Boost Workplace Productivity—Make 'Em Laugh!" Lazy Fairy Improv, accessed November 1, 2012, http://www.lazyfairy improv.com/blog/boost-workplace-productivity-make-em-laugh.

5. "H. Jackson Brown Jr. Quotes," goodreads, accessed November 1, 2016, http://www.goodreads.com/quotes/7992-don-t-say-you-don-t-have-enough-time-you-have-exactly.

6. "M'Cheyne Quotations," The Robert Murray M'Cheyne Resource, accessed November 1, 2012, http://www.mcheyne.info/quotes.php.

Chapter 7

1. "Television and Health," Internet Resources to Accompany the Sourcebook for Teaching Science, accessed November 1, 2012, http://www.csun.edu/science/health/docs/tv&health.html.

2. "Memory Changes in Older Adults," American Psychological Association, accessed November 1, 2016, http://www.apa.org/research/action/memory-changes.aspx.

3. Woods Hutchinson, M.D., "Balanced Work," The Saturday Evening Post 194 (1922): 40, accessed October 19, 2016, https://books.google.com/books?id=JCkkAQAAMAAJ&printsec=frontcover#v=onepage&q&f=false.

4. Brad Tuttle, "How Much You Spend Each Year on Coffee, Gas, Christmas, Pets, Beer, and More," Time, accessed November 1, 2012, http://business.time.com/2012/01/23/howmuch-you-spend-each-year-on-coffee-gaschristmas-pets-beer-and-more/.

Chapter 8

1. Helena Zhu, "Weight of the World: Adult Population Weighs 633 Billion Pounds," The Epoch Times, June 20, 2012, accessed November 1, 2012, http://printarchive.epochtimes.com/a1/en/us/sfo/2012/06-Jun/21/B3_20120621_NoCA-US.pdf.

2. "Stadium Comparison," New York Yankees, accessed November 1, 2016, http://newyork.yankees.mlb.com/nyy/ballpark/new_stadium_comparison.jsp.

3. Hagopian Institute, comp., *Quote Junkie Funny Edition* (Hagopian Institute, 2008), 120.

4. Matt Walker, "Sleep: Expert Q and A," NOVA, July 2007, http://www.pbs.org/wgbh/nova/body/walker-sleep.html.

Chapter 9

1. Ralph Waldo Emerson, Alfred Riggs Ferguson, Glen M. Johnson, *The Collected Works of Ralph Waldo Emerson: Letters and Social Aims* (Cambridge, MA: Harvard University Press, 2010), 50.

2. Clyde E. Nichols, *Lift Up Your Eyes: Devotions for Every Day of the Year* (Bloomington, IN: AuthorHouse, 2011), 307.

3. "Grimm's Fairy Tales: The Frog Prince," Lit2Go, accessed November 1, 2016, http://etc.usf.edu/lit2go/175/grimms-fairy-tales/3066/the-frog-prince/.

Chapter 10

1. "George Bernard Shaw—A Splendid Torch," Not Always On, accessed November 1, 2016, http://www.elise.com/quotes/george_bernard_shaw_-_a_splendid_torch.

2. Ed Tandy McGlasson, "What Difference Will You Make this Year?" Fathers Coaching Newsletter, accessed November 1, 2012, http://www.edtandymcglasson.org/.

3. John Sedgwick, "Lost Children," Best Life, May 2006, http://www.businesswire.com/news/home/20060511005630/en/Life-Magazine-Devotes-June-2006-Issue-Fathers.

4. Randy Wilson, "Develop Emotional Intimacy with Your Kids," Focus on the Family, accessed November 1, 2012, http://www.focusonthefamily.com/parenting/building_relationships/celebrating_your_family_identity/develop_emotional_intimacy_with_your_kids.aspx.

CPSIA information can be obtained
at www.ICGtesting.com
Printed in the USA
FSOW03n0129070717
36041FS